The No-Prep Bible Study Series

Happiness
vs.
Purpose

What People Are Saying

You can always count on Kenny to provide rich resources that facilitate engaging Bible studies. *Happiness vs. Purpose* will stretch your thinking about what really matters and what doesn't. This 5-week study will bless your soul and foster greater fulfillment in your life.

—Dr. Raymond McHenry, Lead Pastor, Westgate
Memorial Baptist Church, Beaumont, Texas

After using many other Bible study materials with my women's group, I finally discovered The *No-Prep Bible Study Series*. Every book in this series is written in an engaging and easy-to-use format that we didn't experience in with any other bible study. The women in our group have loved each and every book and our understanding of the Bible has grown tremendously.

—Beth Crawford, Minnesota

Happiness vs. Purpose is the third *No-Prep Bible Study* I have taken my Small Group through. Just like the first two booklets, I found it extremely easy to teach and to have participation from the members. Everyone in my Small Group has enjoyed these all studies immensely. Keep the booklets coming Kenny!

—John McMahon, Fulshear, Texas

Happiness vs. Purpose is a great booklet for small group Bible studies. The format is so easy to use! Several different people in our group led the lessons quite handily. But the best thing about Kenny's books is that the lessons make for deep discussions. They just don't cover soft issues, but bring theological truth to bear on the things we face in everyday life.

—Jimmy Taylor, Pastor of Spiritual Formations, Westland
Baptist Church, Katy Texas

The No-Prep
Bible Study Series

Happiness
vs.
Purpose

Kenny Beck

Dedication

To the "In Christ Alone" Adult Bible Fellowship

Contents

Acknowledgements

Special thanks have to go first to my wife, Melissa, and daughter, Mallory. These two highly talented ladies have handled all the editing, layout, and artwork for this book. What you hold in your hands exists because of their ideas and handiwork.

Additionally, I'd like to give a quick nod to one Bible teacher in particular: Mark Lanier. I've absorbed a certain biblical perspective and viewpoint from listening online to Mark's world-renowned teaching in his long-running Biblical Literacy Class at Champion Forest Baptist Church of Houston.

Finally, I must mention three pastors who have had a major impact on my spiritual life: the late Dr. John R. Bisagno, Ryan Rush, and Roy Meadows. All three of these men have inspired my spirit, enlightened my mind, and been a shining personal example to me.

The No-Prep Bible Study Series

The *No-Prep Bible Study Series* is designed to meet the needs of the untold thousands of small groups engaged in Bible study. They are known in the church world as Community Groups, Life Groups, Small Groups, Adult Bible Fellowships, and even by the old-fashioned name of, yes, Sunday School Classes.

By "no prep," we mean no preparation on the part of the **leader or the participants**. You can simply read the short text, answer the questions, and bring a **meaningful and focused** Bible study to conclusion in 45 minutes.

These studies are geared for Christians across denominational lines. Indeed, every study has been trial tested on real small groups from different denominations. Participants have invariably found these unique studies to be engaging and thought provoking.

Group Tips

- Your group should designate a leader to be in charge of three things:
    - Starting on time
    - Keeping it moving
    - Finishing on time

- Always check the given answers to make sure you stay on track.
- Be kind and don't let one person dominate.
- Budget 45 minutes and stick to it!

We pray that God blesses you and speaks to you as you study *Happiness vs. Purpose*.

Also Available

- *Jesus' Most Popular Parables*
- *The Most Glorious Psalms Ever*

Coming Soon

- *I Love to Tell the Story*
- *This Changes Everything!*
- *Our Really Big Family: The Sheptock Story*

Translations Available

- Spanish—*Las Parábolas Más Populares de Jesús*
- Mandarin—*Jesus' Most Popular Parables*
- Mandarin—*The Most Glorious Psalms Ever*

Check for availability at either:

- Amazon.com
- NoPrepBibleStudies.com

A Quick Word About
Happiness and Purpose

Where's the Happiness Part?

Most folks are a little shocked and somewhat disappointed when I tell them that the topic of happiness is not in the Bible.

The words "happy" and "happiness" barely make a dent in your Bible's concordance. And "happiness" is nowhere to be found in the "find-some-verses-on-this-topic" section found at the beginning of many Bibles.

For instance, here's a smattering of "H" topics found in my New Living Translation Bible: hatred, holiness, honesty, hope, hospitality, humility, hypocrisy. Happiness didn't make the list. Hmm. The most basic human pursuit—happiness—seems to be missing in action.

Could this lack of biblical visibility for happiness be telling us something? Perhaps. Famous missionary wife, Elisabeth Elliott once said: "The fact is, as a believer, it is not about me. It is not about my happiness. It is about the glory of God and the kingdom of Christ". Maybe Elisabeth is right. Maybe it isn't all about our happiness. The Bible itself certainly seems silent on the subject.

Where's the Purpose Part?

The good news is that the Bible does tell us our purpose in life. The bad news is that it doesn't just out and out say it. Wouldn't it be nice to have a verse that clearly says, "Your purpose in life is blah, blah, blah."

That's okay. There are some strong commands of Christ that give us our ultimate purpose as Christ followers. We just have to find them.

What Really Matters in Life?

Extremely close on the heels of finding our purpose in life is determining what really matters. Indeed, our purpose and what matters are inextricably intertwined. We will definitively address what is important in life and what is not in Chapter 4, "Double Check Your Calling."

But before you get started in this booklet, here's a rather sobering quote from Francis Chan that I ran across recently: "Our greatest fear should not be of failure, but of succeeding at things in life that don't really matter." Wow Francis! You certainly put us on notice!

May God bless you as you contemplate what God's word tells us about our purpose and doing what matters most.

1

The Pursuit
of Happiness

Focal Verses

Hebrews 13:16 (ESV)

Do not neglect to do good and to share what you have, for such sacrifices are pleasing to God.

Acts 10:42 (ESV)

And he commanded us to preach to the people and to testify that he is the one appointed by God to be judge of the living and the dead.

The Study

An American Right

Here are perhaps the most recognizable words in all of American history.

> *We hold these truths to be self-evident, that all men are created equal, that they are endowed by their Creator, with certain unalienable Rights, that among these are Life, Liberty, and the pursuit of Happiness.*

Yes, that is the monumental second sentence from The Declaration of Independence. It almost has a biblical ring to it. And it certainly appeals to us! God gives you **your life**. Your country should guarantee **your freedom**. And then it is simply up to you to go for it and **shoot for happiness.** Doesn't that sound good, right, and logical?

By and large, Americans have readily embraced the pursuit of happiness as their main goal in life. Some have thought it through. Many, however, have not. To be on the safe side, maybe we should double check this pursuit of happiness thing just to make sure we are on the correct path.

I would posit to you that there are essentially two approaches people take in shooting for happiness. I've dubbed them "Man's Formula" and "God's Formula." As you might guess, "God's Formula" might be a tad better. Let's go ahead take a quick look both formulas.

Man's Formula

America today is a very wealthy place and the siren call to happiness usually travels smack dab through our riches. Almost without thinking, the pursuit of happiness formula usually ends up being this:

Buy things that give you pleasure

1. Name 5 big-ticket items that Americans purchase in an effort to be happy.

2. Name 5 lesser items that Americans buy that give them pleasure.

Of course, the formula of us buying things to make us happy is clearly an oversimplification. We definitely do plenty of other things that bring us pleasure. Indeed, French fashion guru Coco Chanel once famously said, "The best things in life are free."

3.   Name 5 things you can enjoy that are free.

Nevertheless, most Americans do make a full frontal assault on happiness, shooting for it by trying to acquire more and better things. Here now is the full Coco Chanel quote, "The best things in life are free. The second best things are very, very expensive." Thanks for your view, Coco!

Basically, everything in our modern society is screaming at us that we'll be happy if we have the best things and experiences this world can offer. It is a deception.

God's Formula

You will most likely build your life around one of these two plans:

- Doing what makes you happy
- Finding and doing your God-given purpose

If you choose to go the "purpose" route, your pursuit of happiness formula might be described this way:

Do God's purpose for your life

which brings you fulfillment

which leads to happiness

I think you noticed that keyword—fulfillment. Ultimately you are seeking **fulfillment and meaning** for your life. And you will only find that fulfillment in doing what God has designed you to do. Happiness ends up being the by-product of finding and doing God's purpose for your life.

Star Houston Astro baseball player, Lance Berkman, once put it this way, "It's only in service to God that you'll find lasting fulfillment."

Hmmm. Lasting fulfillment (and thereby happiness) found only in service to God? I think Lance is on to something—at least more so than Coco Chanel!

For today, let's quickly zero in on just two big-picture purposes that God gives each and every Christian—two purposes that theoretically should lead to fulfillment and subsequent happiness—if we do them!

God-Given Purpose #1

The book of Hebrews is a long, but fairly typical New Testament epistle in that it follows the standard template of "theology first, ethics second." First, there are 12 glorious theological chapters focusing on the superiority of Christ. Then Chapter 13 gets practical with some concluding ethical exhortations.

Read Hebrews 13:16.

Looks like we just found God-given purpose #1—**sharing what we have!** And "what we have" can quickly be defined as our time, talent, and treasure. But notice how our sharing is framed as **sacrifices**.

Sacrifice isn't a popular word in the go-go world of today. It means you give up something—usually something valuable!

In baseball, when a batter bunts while trying to move a runner over, it is called a sacrifice bunt. The batter is giving himself up. He is out. The runner is advanced.

As a Christian, when you give up your time, talent, or treasure for someone else, that is **sacrificing for others**. You are out some of your time, talent, or treasure. Other people are advanced and served. And the Lord is pleased with you, His sacrificial servant!

The first place we should look for folks to make some sacrifices for is inside our families.

4. Who in your family isn't self-sufficient and needs your help?

The second place we should look is outside our families. Christians typically band together into organizations to help every kind of people in need.

5.   Name some local organizations and what they do to help needy people.

6.   Name some worldwide organizations and what they do to help needy people.

Sacrificing for others through Christian organizations is a great way to obey Jesus' rather blunt instruction in Luke 12:33, "Sell your possessions and give to the needy."

7.   How fulfilling has **sacrificing for others** been in your life?

God-Given Purpose #2

In Acts 10, Peter heads off to Caesarea to preach the gospel to a certain Roman centurion named Cornelius. Peter's sermon starts in v. 34, and he doesn't beat around the bush. Peter preaches Jesus from the get-go arriving at the core of the gospel—the death, burial, and resurrection of Christ by v. 39.

Then in v. 42, Peter says something in passing that clues us in to our God-given purpose #2.

Read Acts 10:42.

Let's focus on the just first 9 words of that verse beginning with the important task of defining the pronouns.

8.   Who is "he?"

9.   Who is "us?"

Hmmm. Peter said that Jesus **commanded** the disciples to preach the gospel to all people. I prefer the New American Standard's translation here even more: "and he **ordered** us to preach to the people." Wow. It seems that Jesus literally **gave orders** for his disciples to spread the word about His death, burial, and resurrection.

Those "orders" came on the Mount of Olives right before Jesus ascended.

10. What were the disciples "ordered" to do in Acts 1:8?

11. Where were the disciples "ordered" to go in Acts 1:8?

12. Bonus points: What famous phrase did Jesus use in Matthew 4:19 that strongly hints of an evangelistic purpose for all followers of Christ?

Let's check a few places in Acts to see if Christ's followers did indeed follow His orders.

13. What was Phillip busy doing in Acts 8:5?

14. What were Peter and John doing in Acts 8:25?

15. What did Paul do right after his conversion in Acts 9:20?

Wow. It looks like every follower of Christ in Acts is running around **proclaiming Christ!**

We will flesh out the various ways that we can personally **proclaim Christ** nowadays in Study #5. But for now, I think we can fairly say that Christ's command for us to **proclaim Him** is a strong God-given purpose #2. I mean, Jesus **ordered** us to do it. It's that simple.

A Final Word

One of the most popular Christian books ever written is *The Purpose Driven Life* by Rick Warren[1]. I highly recommend it. I'm going to let Rick have the final say today. Here's his incisive final words from *The Purpose Driven Life:*

> ***Living with purpose is the only way to really live.***
>
> ***Everything else is just existing.***

Very true, Pastor Rick!

Finding and doing God's purpose for our lives should be the starting point in our pursuit of happiness. And the two God-givien purposes we laid out in our study today—sacrificing for others and proclaiming Christ—are likely the biggest purposes you can build your life around.

My Answers

Question 1

Houses and ranches, cars and trucks, smart phones, big-screen TVs, grand pianos

Question 2

Vacations, cruises, fine dining, sporting events, movies

Question 3

A beautiful sunset, a friend's smile, a hearty laugh, a finished task, a new PR in the marathon, a cold water fountain on your walking trail

Question 4

People needing help inside your family could be: your 3-year-old child, your 93-year-old grandmother, your 33-year-old adult child with special needs

Question 5

Most areas have at least a food bank, a homeless shelter, a crisis pregnancy center, etc.

Question 6

Compassion International—helps poor children around the globe

Living Water International—digs water wells in Latin America

Samaritan's Purse—most every emergency need imaginable

International Justice Mission—rescues girls from sex trafficking

Question 7

Most folks tend to say that they experience the most meaning and fulfillment of their lives when they are doing things sacrificially for others.

Question 8

He = Jesus

Question 9

Us = the original 12 disciples

Question 10

The disciples were "ordered" to be witnesses of Christ

Question 11

The disciples were "ordered" to be witnesses for Christ, first in Jerusalem, then in Judea and Samaria, and then to the ends of the earth. Of course, the original 12 disciples couldn't cover the whole world. That is *our* job.

Question 12

Famous phrase = "Fishers of men." Evangelism seems to have been on Jesus' mind when he called the disciples. Contrarily, Jesus didn't say, "Hey guys, follow Me and we will have some fun and eat some banana splits all over Galilee."

Question 13

Proclaiming Christ

Question 14

Preaching the gospel

Question 15

Proclaiming Jesus

2

The Deceitfulness
of Riches

Focal Verses

Matthew 13:22 (ESV)

As for what was sown among thorns, this is the one who hears the word, but the cares of the world and the deceitfulness of riches choke the word, and it proves unfruitful.

1 Timothy 6:9 (ESV)

But those who desire to be rich fall into temptation, into a snare, into many senseless and harmful desires that plunge people into ruin and destruction.

The Study

Shooting For Happiness

Last lesson we postulated that people usually pursue happiness in one of two ways.

The typical way is the basic frontal assault. Just go for it! Essentially, it boils down to **buying things that bring you pleasure**. Here's quick set of questions to help evaluate that plan.

1. How happy do you feel **the day** you get a new car?

2. How happy do you feel **one month** later?

3. How happy do you feel **one year** later?

Hmm. Seems like happiness, at best, is a fleeting thing when it is tied to having nice things that you get used to over time.

The second approach in pursuing happiness brings God into the picture. It involves **doing God's purpose for your life**. This brings fulfillment. And fulfillment brings lasting happiness, or what we might call joy.

Of course, many folks insist on choosing plan A, the frontal assault plan—because buying more and better toys is the American way!

But there are Scriptures that warn us about what lies down that path. One of those little warning verses is sneakily buried in a very familiar parable. You may have never noticed it!

The Parable of the Sower

"The Parable of the Sower" almost made it into our first book—*Jesus' Most Popular Parables*. Most Christians know and love this parable which, quite surprisingly, is in all three synoptic Gospels!

You recall what happens. The sower throws out seed onto four different soils.

- The hard path
- The rocky soil
- The soil with thorns
- The good soil

Only the seed sown on the good soil ends up producing any fruit. And that is the main point. Christ explains that you don't want to be like any of those first three soils, which produce nothing for the kingdom. You want to be like that last soil—the good soil—which is very productive for the Lord.

That is the overall context as we jump right in to what Christ says about that third soil—the soil with lots of thorns.

A Sneaky Verse on Deception

Read Matthew 13:22.

4. What two things does Jesus say the thorns represent?

5. What do those two things actually do? (**one main verb**)

6. And what is the result?

So, Christ is essentially saying that worldly cares and the pursuit of riches tends to crowd out doing productive things for His kingdom. Ouch!

2 The Deceitfulness of Riches

It could conceivably be boiled down to this killer phrase:

A life of pleasure

crowds out

a life of purpose

Contemplate that carefully.

If we make our lives primarily about pursuing happiness through pleasurable experiences, then there just isn't much time and energy left for doing things for the Lord—the things He calls us to do. We simply have to choose our main focus. Either we **focus on our pleasure** or **we focus on our purpose.**

The central take-away of this parable is: We don't want the pursuit of pleasure to detract us from doing the Lord's assignments.

In the middle of all this, it is very easy to overlook the sneaky phrase: "**the deceitfulness of riches.**" Go back and circle that phrase in the text. That phrase seems to imply that some sort deception factor is involved with riches. We'd better explore that further. A lot further.

Defining Deception

The word "deceitfulness" really catches my attention. The root word is "deceive." A quick look-up of synonyms for "deceive" produces: "swindle," "defraud," "cheat," "trick," "dupe." Whoa! Are you getting the feeling that pursuing riches may not be a good thing? Maybe riches aren't simply innocuous. Maybe they are downright fraudulent.

"Deceive" is such a highly abstract word that we probably could use a full sentence to help us understand it better. Here's one:

When something deceives you

it promises one thing

but delivers the opposite

Hmmm. Promises one thing…but delivers the opposite.

7.   What do you think about this expanded definition of "deceive?"

Let's play a fun little word association game that I'll call "The Deceiving Game." Below is a list of four words associated with four different animals that human beings routinely deceive. Identify each animal and then say what happens to it.

8. Lure—

9. Feed corn—

10. Decoy—

11. Cheese—

Yes, we humans can certainly deceive the animal kingdom. We deceive that little fishy in the lake with a lure that enticingly says, "Here's some dinner for you, when are really we are planning on eating that little fishy for dinner. Sure seems like "promising one thing, and delivering the opposite."

Here's a real-life human deception story. Many years ago, I read about this notorious lady dubbed "Banana Pudding Lilly." One day, Lilly sweetly served her husband his favorite desert, banana pudding…after lacing it with arsenic. Now there's a serious case of "promising one thing, and delivering the opposite."

Maybe, just maybe, we ought to approach the pursuit of riches as cautiously as we should approach "Banana Pudding Lilly."

Here's why. **A full-throated pursuit of happiness through pleasure does not result in happiness.** It results in unfulfillment. And unfulfillment results in unhappiness. It promises one thing and delivers the opposite!

Another Sneaky Verse on Deception

See if you can fill in blanks on this very familiar Bible verse.

12. The _____ of _____ is the root of all evil.

Seems like most folks know that verse. It is 1 Timothy 6:10. But not many people know the immediate prior verse.

Read 1 Timothy 6:9.

13. What specific word in this verse has overtones of deceit and deception?

Circle that word in the text. Some translations go with the word "trap" instead of "snare." Both are good. The underlying Greek word-picture is one of a dug-out pit in the ground, covered with leaves, with sharp stakes at the bottom. Another deceptive animal trap, if you will.

14. What does this verse say is the result of falling into the trap of pursuing riches?

Again, we have the same broad sequence of thought: Going after riches and pleasures doesn't make us happy. It is a deception. **The result is not merely unhappiness, but ruin and destruction.** This is not the path to take!

One Man's Testimony

Countless people have testified that their acquired riches and pleasures did not bring them fulfillment and happiness. But one man is particularly noteworthy on this front: King Solomon.

Here's the way Solomon expressed it in Ecclesiastes 5:10 (NLT):

Those who love money will never have enough.

How absurd to think

that wealth brings true happiness!

Solomon is right. Pleasure and wealth do not bring lasting happiness. True fulfillment and lasting happiness is only found in doing what God has called you to do.

May you and I choose the path of purpose over pleasure!

My Answers

Question 1

You are probably on cloud nine the day you get a new car—whether it's a new Cadillac or a used Toyota.

Question 2

A month later, your cloud-nine feelings have likely dissipated (maybe down to cloud five), but at least that new car smell still lingers in the air.

Question 3

A year later, you've gotten used to that car. It is no longer new to you, and likely your happy feelings have melted away like a snow-cone on a hot day.

Question 4

- The cares of the world
- The deceitfulness of riches

Question 5

Key verb = choke; meaning choke out or crowd out

Question 6

Result = no fruit; the seed ended up producing nothing

Question 7

I like this expanded definition of "deceive." It seems to break "deceive" down into its two logical component parts.

Question 8

Fish—Small fish get thrown back. But, if they are big enough, they become dinner.

Question 9

Deer—If you are a young deer, you are probably okay. If you are a female deer, you are probably okay. If you are a male deer, you are definitely not okay.

Question 10

Duck— From watching Duck Dynasty, I've learned that decoys are set out on the water to tell the ducks flying overhead, "Hey, this looks like a good place to land." Then when the ducks get low enough, the Robertsons' guns start booming. And then Miss Kay fixes duck for dinner.

Question 11

Mouse—When the mouse takes the cheese in that mousetrap, well, I'll just let you use your imagination

Question 12

The love of money is the root of all evil (1 Timothy 6:10)

Question 13

"Snare" implies deceit and deception

Question 14

Result = ruin and destruction

3

The Four
Callings

Focal Verses

Galatians 1:15-16 (NIV)

But when God, who set me apart from my mother's womb and **called me** by his grace, was pleased to reveal his Son in me . . .

1 Thessalonians 4:7 (NLT)

God has **called us** to live holy lives, not impure lives.

Acts 13:2 (ESV)

While they were worshiping the Lord and fasting, the Holy Spirit said, "Set apart for me Barnabas and Saul for the work to which I have **called them**."

Acts 16:10 (ESV)

And when Paul had seen the vision, immediately we sought to go on into Macedonia, concluding that God had **called us** to preach the gospel to them.

The Study

Today's Quest

Over the first two lessons, we proposed that the best road to finding happiness is not by acquiring things that bring you pleasure, but by doing your God-given purpose. Granted, that is still a very broad thought. But today we are going to get way more specific.

Finding your God-given purpose means finding God's specific calling for your life. Yes, God calls you to do some very specific things to further His kingdom. When you do what you are called to do, your life has meaning. And that brings a certain fulfillment. And the final result is likely a lasting happiness.

The scriptures speak of four different callings that God has for your life. Your quest today is to fill in the following chart as we go through those four callings, and to challenge yourself in each area.

The Four Callings

1. *Get* _____
2. *Be* _____
3. *Do* _____
4. *Go* _____

Calling #1

Read Galatians 1:15-16.

In this passage, the apostle Paul is giving his testimony about when God **called him** to salvation. And that is what Calling #1 is—**get saved!**

Paul's salvation experience is described at length in Acts 9.

1. Exactly where did Paul get saved per Acts 9:3?

2. What time of day did Paul get saved per Acts 22:6?

Many times, but not always, a person gets saved by believing in Christ at a very specific time and place that they can readily recall. I can remember believing in Jesus Christ as my Lord and Savior in the pastor's office at FBC Beaumont in 1967. C.S. Lewis famously said that he was saved on a bus going to the London zoo.

3.   Tell about where and when you first believed in Christ as your Savior.

Christ's personal call for people to believe in Him is so unmistakably clear throughout the gospel of John—no place more so than John 14:1, "You believe in God, believe also in Me." Make doubly sure that you've responded to this paramount first calling—believe in Him!

Calling #2

Read 1 Thessalonians 4:7.

In this verse, Paul says point blank that **God calls us** to live holy lives. That is Calling #2—**be holy.**

When you read all 13 of Paul's NT epistles, you notice a trend. Paul tends to teach "theology first, ethics second." So, towards the end of many of Paul's letters you find lists—usually two lists. A list of sinful old behaviors that Christians should rid themselves of. And a list of virtuous new behaviors that Christians should incorporate into their life.

Paul is essentially laying out a holiness formula of "out with the old, and in with the new." And his favorite term for this process is "renew."

But there are additional words that start with "re" which can help us understand this "out with the old, in with the new" concept. Here's some:

4.   What do Chip and Joanna Gaines do to houses on their popular TV show *Fixer Upper*? (Answers must start with "re.")

5.   What do you do to your computer sometimes when it is wigging out? (Answers must start with "re.")

6. Do you think a Christian's renovation to holiness is usually a long process or a quick process?

Whether you think the process is usually fast or usually slow, the key is to understand that there is a tearing out of old sinful behaviors and replacing them with new virtuous behaviors.

Hopefully you are far enough along the road to holiness that the Lord **can use you now** to get some things done for His glory.

Calling #3

Read Acts 13:2.

In this verse, we find that **God called** Paul and Barnabas to do some specific "work." That is Calling #3—**do something!** In their case, Paul and Barnabas were called to leave their cushy lives in Antioch, and go get beaten and flogged while evangelizing a massive section of the Roman Empire.

You and I probably won't be called to such a mammoth task. But, every Christian is definitely called to **do something** for God's kingdom. In fact, God designed you and gave you certain strengths to do the thing he calls you to do!

And that something could be absolutely anything!

One of my all time favorite books is *God's Smuggler* by Brother Andrew[2]. I highly recommend it. Andrew smuggled Bibles into Eastern European Communist countries back in the day when Bibles were forbidden there. Did he ever get caught? You'll have to read the book. But smuggling Bibles was clearly Brother Andrew's calling.

Here are 10 Christians that I know personally who would tell you they've found their current calling. Some are on a church staff. Most are not.

* God's Preacher—Scooter W
* God's Pilot—Marty G
* God's VBS teacher—Christy R
* God's Water Well Driller—Kevin E

- God's Singer—Betty A
- God's Disaster Recovery Specialist—Mark S
- God's Prison Minister—John W
- God's Sunday School Teacher—Bert B
- God's Muslim Specialist—Sylvia E
- God's Homeschool Specialist—Brandi C

There's a serious story of service and calling behind each of those very real names.

7. Has God already called you to do something? What?

If you figure out **the exact something the Lord has called you to do**, you will likely experience what I call the four C's—clarity about what to do, conviction to do it, courage while doing it, and contentment when you've done it. Those are some powerful C's. Make the effort to find and do the specific something He's called you to do!

And don't be afraid to label yourself as "God's Whatever." It's a trick that will help keep you on track mentally.

Calling #4

Read Acts 16:10.

This verse houses the most famous call in the NT. The Lord called the missionary team of Paul, Silas, Luke, and Timothy to cross the Aegean Sea and take the Gospel to the next big land mass to the west—Greece. That's what calling #4 is—**go somewhere!**

Through the centuries, God has called Christians to go certain places. And He still does today!

On Wednesday night, January 26, 1983, I was participating in adult choir practice at one of the biggest churches in Houston. Towards the end, the Lord unmistakably told me to go and play the organ for free at a very small church in the west Houston suburb of Katy. Three days later on Saturday, I went and tested their Baldwin organ. The pastor overheard my playing, came charging into the sanctuary, and said, "Whoever you are, you're starting here tomorrow!"

Long story short, I've been a piano teacher and Sunday School teacher in Katy ever since.

8. Has God ever told you to go somewhere?

One Last Crucial Thing

So, we found these "The Four Callings" in Scripture:

- Get saved
- Be holy
- Do something
- Go somewhere

But here's one final crucial thing: Do them in order! Believe it or not, some folks blow it and get things way out of order.

Joanne Sheptock got things out of order in her life. She and her husband Rudy adopted and raised 50 children over some 40 years. And not just any kids—extreme special needs kids.

The only thing was, Joanne was never saved to begin with.

About 20 years into this humongous parenting task, Joanne went to a ladies Bible study. The ladies were studying the "Sermon on the Mount," when Matthew 5:16 bopped her on the head. "Let your light shine before men, so that they may see your good works and glorify your Father who is in heaven." It stopped Joanne in her tracks because she was quite certain that her good works should bring glory to herself, not some entity called "the Father."

It dawned on Joanne that she did not know Christ. She immediately accepted the Lord as her Savior—Calling #1. Then she kept right on going with her adoptive parenting—Calling #3.

So be careful. Don't make Joanne's initial mistake.

Make doubly sure you do all "The Four Callings" in order!

My Answers

Question 1

On the road to Damascus—in fact he was almost there

Question 2

About noon—Paul's testimony was very specific as to time of day

Question 3

Your own experience

Question 4

Renovate, refurbish, renew, revamp, rebuild—I think renovation is the best analogy for "out with the old, in with the new." In *Fixer Upper*, Chip first tears out all the old crummy stuff in the house. Then the new construction projects flesh out the house again. Finally, Joanna decorates it to the nines.

Question 5

Restart, reboot

Question 6

I personally feel like the Lord works the holiness "renovation" on a new Christian fairly fast. Of course, ultimately it is a life-long process that is never 100% complete. But, on average, those obvious horrible sinful things are ripped out of our lives by the Lord in a few months, or year or two—not 40 years! Think of it this way—the destruction phase in home renovation is fast, the rebuild is a medium length, the beautification and decoration is always ongoing.

Question 7

What God has already called you to do

Question 8

Where God has already called you to go

4

Double Check
Your Calling

Focal Verse

Ecclesiastes 3:11b (NIV)

He has also set eternity in the human heart.

The Study

It's in Your Heart

In our first lesson, we proposed that the best way to find happiness in this life is to seek lasting fulfillment in doing our God-given purpose. Basically, our purpose, or calling, is the thing that God calls us to do to further His kingdom.

Since this is so critical, maybe, just maybe, we ought to double check our calling to make totally sure we are on the right track.

Here's the focal verse for today. It holds the key to double checking your calling.

Read Ecclesiastes 3:11b.

This verse says that **God has given you an eternal perspective.**

It means you desire to live your life for things of eternal significance. In other words, you want your life to count for eternity!

And that is the sieve you need to run your perceived calling through—eternity. Your God-given calling should have some sort of eternal impact.

Therefore, it would be good to remind ourselves exactly what things are **eternal**, and what things are **temporary**.

Let's jump into the weeds immediately. Let's make a list of seven things that you have which are temporary and another list of three things that you have which are eternal.

Your Temporary List

Many of these things will be obvious. But it is good to review them. Plus, you might not have thought about a couple of things on this list.

Thing one—your body. There are two parts to you—your body and your soul. Your physical body is definitely temporary. It will age. It will die. It will return to dust. We like to think we will live forever and be forever young. But your body comes with an expiration date—70 years, 90 years, maybe 100 years.

1.   What do we do to make our bodies last a little longer?

Thing two—your stuff. I can safely say that every object you own will eventually disintegrate and be reduced to powder. 2 Peter 3:10-12 says that the world as we know it is going to be burnt up at the end of time. I know one preacher who tries to drive this point home by advising people to write "Temporary" on a bunch of yellow post-it notes and put them on everything they own.

2.   Name five things that you own won't make it into eternity.

Thing three—your animals. Yep. Your cats and dogs and horses will wear out even faster than you will. They aren't eternal.

Thing four—your job. In the olden days, people tended to work just one job till they retired. Nowadays, jobs go "poof" all the time. Either via "retirement" or "poof," you won't be working your job 100 years from now.

3.   What is your current job that won't last forever?

Thing five—your marriage. I'm not predicting a divorce for you. I'm simply saying what Jesus said in Matthew 22:30. Jesus said nobody is married in heaven. Marriages are over, kaput!

But not all religions teach "no-marriages-in-heaven."

4.   What major religion teaches that **their special** "sealed celestial marriages" on this earth will last "for time and all eternity?"

That particular religion is obviously going against the Jesus' words on this issue. Marriages simply aren't eternal. They are temporary. Maybe that fact makes you sad. But then again, maybe it makes you just a little bit glad.

Thing six—your country. Sorry to say, but countries come and countries go. No country is eternal. Even Texas won't last forever. Now that is sad!

Thing seven—your planet. Truth be told, planet earth—our "Home, Sweet, Home"—is not eternal. Whether you believe the earth is six-thousand years old, or six-billion years old, it is a certainty (both scientifically and biblically) that it will not last forever.

Now that we've preached doom and gloom establishing the temporary nature of almost everything, let's move on to happier thoughts. Let's briefly contemplate what is eternal.

Your Eternal List

Thing one—your soul. Yes. Your soul, that invisible part of you, the real you, it is eternal. Your soul is the part of you that will last forever.

Thing two—your eternal destiny. In several places, the Bible teaches two eternal destinies. First and foremost, you want to make sure your soul ends up in heaven for eternity. Accept Christ without delay!

Thing three—your eternal rewards. We sometimes forget that there are eternal rewards for Christians who've done things for the Lord. Those rewards will not wear out. They will be forever. Paul speaks about eternal rewards in 1 Cor 3:14 and 2 Cor 5:10.

But mainly wrap your mind around this. Your eternal rewards will be based on what you do for other people! When you sacrifice for others, your treasure builds up in heaven. Jesus makes this connection abundantly clear in Luke 12:33 (NLT):

> *Sell your possessions and give to those in need. This will store up treasure for you in heaven! And the purses of heaven never get old or develop holes. Your treasure will be safe; no thief can steal it and no moth can destroy it.*

So, you have but three eternal things—your soul, your eternal destiny, and your eternal rewards.

Double Check These "Callings"

It is now time to double check some possible callings. With a good grip on what is eternal and what is temporary, we can better see what activities might have an eternal impact.

I've listed below six real people doing real activities. Your assignment is to make a judgement call on whether or not you think the "good" activity could be a God-given calling that has an eternal impact.

Ed and Glenda H—Foster-parented many children. These foster children received the same Christian upbringing as their regular kids.

5.   God-given calling with an **eternal impact**?

Doris D—Prominent animal welfare activist (mostly for dogs) in Los Angeles for 50 years. Started and gave millions of dollars to several pet foundations.

6.   God-given calling with an **eternal impact?**

Rudra S—Leaves his home in Calcutta for several months each year. Travels to the most remote and worst part of India to meet needs and preach Christ to an unreached people group.

7.   God-given calling with an **eternal impact?**

Greta T—Teenage Swedish environmental activist trying to get everybody to reduce their carbon footprint, thereby saving the planet.

8.   God-given calling with an **eternal impact**?

Morris B—Took dinner nightly to an aging relative for several years. Stayed for conversation to combat the relative's physical isolation.

9. God-given calling with an **eternal impact?**

Bob and Betty C—Worked tirelessly and gave generously in the '80s and '90s to turn Texas from a blue state to a red state.

10. God-given calling with an **eternal impact?**

We are likely to have differing opinions on some of these "good" activities. Nevertheless, this is a great way to double check your calling. Always ask yourself the question: "Does my calling have any eternal impact?" If not, it may be time to re-evaluate.

A Quick Final Word

One of my all-time favorite Christian books is John Ortberg's *When The Game Is Over, It All Goes Back In The Box*[3]. Dynamite title. Dynamite book. I'm going to let John have the final say today. From page 31:

> *Wise people build their lives around what is eternal,*
>
> *and squeeze in what is temporary.*

Let's be wise people.

Life can get so full of temporary things. We need to double check our calling and concentrate our efforts on things that are truly eternal.

My Answers

Question 1

Exercise, eat right, take supplements, have surgeries

Question 2

Your car, your roof, your favorite chair, your clothes, your beach house (The very humble Beck/Butler beach house was wiped clean away during hurricane Ike in 2008. That's when I really began to understand the word temporary!)

Question 3

I'm a piano teacher. Piano teachers tend not to retire. We tend to teach till we keel over.

Question 4

Mormonism—For those who want an easy-to-grasp insight into Mormonism, I highly recommend the fantastic autobiography *Unveiling Grace* by Lynn Wilder[4]. Lynn's whole family came to faith in Christ after being caught up in Mormonism for 25+ years. Put *Unveiling Grace* on your must-read list. Lynn's story will blow you away. Plus, you'll get an up close and personal look at some of the outlandish doctrines of Mormonism, including "sealed celestial marriages."

Question 5

Yes—Ed and Glenda's foster parenting was indeed their stated "calling" and it clearly had eternal consequences.

Question 6

No—Doris' lifestyle of pronounced animal activism, while indeed a "good thing," regrettably did not have any eternal significance. Animals are on the temporary list. Almost definitionally, **an eternal impact can only be had when helping people.**

Question 7

Yes—Rudra is a one-man missionary wrecking crew, going after perhaps the most impoverished and isolated people group on the planet. The eternal impact this one man is having is almost incalculable.

Question 8

I'm going to have to say no on this one—Greta's "good cause" is definitely noble to herself and noble to lots of folks. But when you get down to brass tacks, our planet is on our temporary list.

Question 9

Yes—This is the typical look of someone making an eternal impact—**one needy person at a time!** By the way, my dad, Morris Beck, took me along on many of these dinner dealies—a dad teaching his son about **sacrificing for others.**

Question 10

No—Any eternal aspects to Bob and Betty's political activism are, at best, **extremely indirect.** And ironically, due to demographics, Texas may gradually turn back into a blue state a mere 30 years later! Bob and Betty's investment of their time and treasure in this "good cause" just seems to come up dry when it comes to eternal significance.

5

The Best Way
to Proclaim Him

Focal Verses

Acts 26:28 (ESV)

And Agrippa said to Paul, "In a short time would you persuade me to be a Christian?"

Hebrews 4:12a (NLT)

For the word of God is alive and powerful. It is sharper than the sharpest two-edged sword.

The Study

That Second Purpose

Way back in our first lesson, we noted two crucial purposes that God gives each and every Christian: **sacrificing for others** and **proclaiming Christ.** Most of this series has dealt with sacrificing for others. But now it is time to flesh out proclaiming Him.

In Acts 1:8, Jesus commanded his followers to go around the world telling everybody about Him. Until Christ returns, that command is still in effect.

But what is the best way for **you personally** to proclaim Him today? I don't know the exact answer. But we are going to quickly lay out today four excellent ways to proclaim Christ. Probably one or two of these ways will resonate in your heart. You'll probably say: "Hey, I can do that one!" You might even enthusiastically say, "Hey, I really want to do that one!"

Whichever one you feel the Lord calling you to do, that is probably the best way for you to proclaim Him.

Way #1—Persuade People

All through Acts, we find Paul preaching sermons to big crowds. But in Acts 26, we see Paul witnessing to just one person, a magistrate named King Agrippa. Paul begins with his testimony, but quickly gets to the heart of Christianity—the death, burial, and resurrection of Christ for the forgiveness of sins. King Agrippa finally gets a word in edgewise in v. 28.

Read Acts 26:28.

You see the key word we are after—**persuade**. King Agrippa correctly felt that Paul was trying to "persuade" him to become a Christian. Apparently, Paul seems to have been an exceptionally persuasive guy. To me, "persuade" carries the perfect sense of what we Christians should be about. We should not be mostly debating or arguing. We should be **persuading people to follow Christ.**

When you think about it, you probably try to persuade someone of something every day. You might try to persuade a co-worker of your idea or your spouse of where to go to dinner or your kids to eat their vegetables. In my life as a piano teacher, I try to persuade parents to sign up their kids for lessons with me instead of another piano teacher down the street.

1. What things do you try to persuade people on?

As to our Christian faith, some of us today should be like the very un-shy apostle Paul. Our mindset should be to persuade people to accept Christ.

2. Do you think every Christian has the gift of persuading others to come to Christ like the Apostle Paul did?

3. Have you ever tried to persuade someone to accept Christ?

Way #2—Challenge People

In 2004, 19-year-old Micah Wilder was doing his two-year Mormon missionary work. While in Orlando, Florida, Micah brazenly attempted to convert a Baptist pastor named Alan Benson to Mormonism. During this bizarre one-hour meeting, Pastor Alan flipped the tables and tried to persuade Micah that Mormonism was a false religion. At the end of this highly contentious meeting, Pastor Alan challenged Micah to simply read the Gospels like a child with no preconceived notions.

For some reason, Micah accepted the challenge and began to read the Gospels like a child. He gradually began to realize that the Jesus of Scriptures was totally different than the Jesus foisted upon him by Mormonism. Micah laid down his works-based Mormon approach to salvation and accepted Christ's free offer of salvation based on grace.

Micah subsequently challenged his girlfriend back in Utah to read the Bible like a child. She too got saved. This challenge to simply read the Gospels like a child ran through Micah's circle of friends and family like wildfire.

When the dust had settled, 14 Mormons had all **totally independently** read the Gospels, been convicted by the Holy Spirit, and had accepted Christ.

One of these 14 saved Mormons was Micah's mother, Lynn Wilder, a professor at BYU in Provo, Utah! You can read about this whole family's stunning conversion in Lynn Wilder's book *Unveiling Grace.*

You see the point. The Gospels themselves are so powerful that people can be saved just by reading and pondering Matthew, Mark, Luke, and John. Perhaps all we need to do is be like Alan Benson and **challenge people to read the Gospels.**

4.   Does challenging people to read the Gospels sound like something you can do?

In today's fast paced world, maybe we should challenge people to read just one Gospel.

5.   Which Gospel might be the best one to challenge someone to read?

All four Gospels are incredibly powerful. You can't make a boo-boo recommending one over another. But clearly, a super strong way to proclaim Christ is to challenge people to read the Gospels.

Way #3—Invite People

Back in my childhood church, the quietest person in our youth group was a guy named Dennis. Truth be told, we kind of picked on Dennis for being so quiet. But Dennis did something **none of the rest of us did.** He invited a friend to church. He invited this guy named Scooter.

Scooter was exposed to the Word of God and quickly accepted Christ. Within a couple of years, Scooter felt the call of the Lord to become a preacher. I will never forget hearing Scooter preach his first sermon at our little church at age 17. Scooter has been a preacher now for 40+ years. No telling how many people have been saved via Scooter preaching the Word.

And all because little ole Dennis invited Scooter to church one day.

The late great pastor of First Baptist Houston, John Bisagno, always encouraged us to bring our friends to church. He said he couldn't do his job in the pulpit if we didn't do our job on the streets.

It really is that simple. A great way to proclaim Christ, is to **invite people to come with you to your church or your small group.**

6. Does inviting people to your church or small group sound like something you can do?

7. Would a person feel more comfortable and more likely to accept an invitation to come to your church or to your small group?

8. Have you ever invited someone to church, a church event, or your small group?

Way #4—Give People

Read Hebrews 4:12a.

You see the key word. The Word of God is **powerful**!

When you get down to brass tacks, God's Word is way more powerful than your testimony or your persuasive skills. And ultimately, your own words only serve to draw people to the story of Jesus Christ in the Gospels anyway.

Perhaps the most basic way to get the Word of God into people's hands is to **just give it to them**. Yes, give them a full Bible, a portion of the Bible, a Bible tract, whatever.

My grandfather W.W. Rangeler was a proud Gideon, lapel pin and all. The Gideons spent millions of their own dollars printing and distributing Bibles. They were best known for placing Gideon Bibles in almost every hotel room across America.

As a piano teacher, I have a waiting area where I put out very readable portions of God's Word. Lots of parents and kids do read and absorb the Word of God there. In my waiting area are:

• All of the *No-Prep Bible Study* booklets, including our Spanish and Mandarin translations—Houston is very diverse!
• Plenty of little Arch Books for children giving them compact Bible stories and parables in rhyme.

So the final way to proclaim Christ might be the easiest. Simply **give people the Word of God.**

9.   Is giving out the Word of God to people something you can do?

10. Have you ever given something biblical to someone?

Wrapping Up

So as this "Happiness v. Purpose" book comes to a close, mull over the best way for you personally to proclaim Christ. No doubt one of these four ways has tugged at your heart and you feel prodded to take some action. Surely one of these verbs has your name on it: **persuade, challenge, invite, give.**

Jesus' final parting marching order was to proclaim Him around the globe. Indeed, it is our main God-given purpose.

My Answers

Question 1

Your answers

Question 2

Not every Christian has the gift of persuasion like the Apostle Paul. Persuasion has a certain "selling" aspect to it. People who are in "sales" tend to be great persuaders. Some folks have that strong "selling" gene. Some do not.

There is a man in my Sunday School class who clearly has the calling to persuade others for Christ at his office. He carefully thinks through his lines of reasoning and persuasion. A great book for people like this is *Tactics* by Greg Koukl[5]. Greg is a professional Christian "debater" who gives you some fabulous ideas on how to engage people using certain probative questions as well as having a very reasonable goal of simply "putting a pebble in someone's shoe."

Question 3

Just off the top of my head, I can recall three people who I tried to persuade to come Christ. All three were clearly impacted. One of them, my high school girlfriend, did accept Christ and became a Methodist pastor.

Question 4

Of course, you can!

Question 5

Every Gospel is a winner! But here are a few considerations.

- Matthew—has the impacting Sermon on the Mount
- Mark—starts fast and is the shortest (which is a plus!)
- Luke—beautiful and cohesive gospel, lots of great parables
- John—some great Jesus stories, presses the reader to believe in Christ

Initial language translations, teaching tools, and videos tend to use either Luke or John. But the quick starting Mark is also used by some.

Question 6

Of course, you can!

Question 7

It all depends on the person. A sociable person might gravitate towards a small group setting. A less social person might prefer coming to a large gathering and not want to interact so closely with people.

Question 8

I have invited lots of folks to both my church and small group. I guess I have the "inviter" gene. It is rare when people take me up on my invitation. But SOMETIMES they do! And invariably, they are blessed, and sometimes they continue coming!

Question 9

Of course, you can!

Question 10

I'm not afraid to give people biblical things. Recently, I gave my auto mechanic named Bruce a copy of *Jesus' Most Popular Parables*. On my next car repair, Bruce told me he read it and loved it.

Addendum

Here's a quick list of five modern people who came to Christ on their own as they read and pondered the Gospels:

> Leonard C. Rosenberg—Jew
>
> Randy Hillebrand—mild atheist
>
> Lynn Wilder—Mormon professor at BYU
>
> J. Warner Wallace—angry atheist
>
> Nabeel Qureshi—rabid Muslim

These folks are what you might call "difficult to convert." No Christian was ever going to persuade them to accept Christ. But the powerful Word of God broke through to each of them. A Google search can lead you to information on each person and their significant Christian ministry.

Notes

1. Rick Warren, *The Purpose Driven Life* (Grand Rapids, MI: Zondervan, 2002).
2. Brother Andrew, *God's Smuggler* (Spire, 1969)
3. John Ortberg, *When the Game is Over, It All Goes Back in the Box* (Grand Rapids, MI: Zondervan, 2007).
4. Lynn Wilder, *Unveiling Grace* (Grand Rapids, MI: Zondervan, 2013).
5. Greg Koukl, *Tactics* (Grand Rapids, MI: Zondervan, 2009).

Statement of Faith

I come from an interdenominational Sunday School teaching family. Among my grandfather, my mother, and me, we've logged some 120 years of teaching across six different denominations. While denominational differences clearly exist, there is a solid theological core to which all Christians readily agree. The following Statement of Faith is proffered as an interdenominational bedrock basis for this book. It is extremely brief and without Scripture references, but certainly represents Christianity at its core.

The Nature of God

- God is creator
- God is holy

The Nature of Man

- Man is created
- Man is born with a sin nature

Man's Situation

- Sin separates man from God
- Man can't extricate himself from his sinful predicament

God' Solution

- God provides a solution for man's sin by the atoning sacrifice of His Son, Jesus Christ on the cross
- Man needs to accept the atoning sacrifice of Christ and believe in His resurrection from the dead

About the Author

Kenny Beck is an adult Bible study teacher with 35 years' experience across three denominations. He has taught every size and age-range of adult Bible classes imaginable.

A typical Kenny Beck lesson features a colorful handout, a huge white dry erase board, a good dollop of class participation, and plenty of enthusiasm.

Vocationally, Kenny has been a full-time private piano teacher in Katy, Texas, since 1984, working with some 40-70 piano students every week.

There are two songs floating around the Christian world written by Kenny and his Nashville pal, Jeff Nelson: "Forever His Blood" and "Take My Life." Both were published by LIFEWAY and are featured on Kenny's piano teacher website: www.kennybeck.com

Feel free to contact Kenny at kennybeck99@gmail.com

He would love to hear from you!

Made in the USA
Columbia, SC
28 January 2025

52900852R00035